IN SEARCH OF PEACE

The Story of Four Americans
Who Won the Nobel Peace Prize

Theodore Roosevelt

Jane Addams

Ralph Bunche

Martin Luther King Jr.

IN SEARCH OF PEACE

The Story of Four Americans Who Won the Nobel Peace Prize

BY ROBERTA STRAUSS FEUERLICHT
Illustrated with photographs

JULIAN MESSNER NEW YORK

Published simultaneously in the United States and Canada by
Julian Messner, a division of Simon & Schuster, Inc.
1 West 39 Street, New York, N.Y. 10018. All rights reserved.

Copyright, ©, 1970 by Roberta Strauss Feuerlicht

Printed in the United States of America
ISBN 0-671-32346-6   Cloth Trade
0-671-32347-4   MCE
Library of Congress Catalog Card No. 70-123165
Design: Majorie Zaum K.

I would like to express my considerable debt to Dr. Ralph Bunche for taking several hours from his crowded schedule to discuss with me the material used in Chapter Three of this book.

Books by Roberta Strauss Feuerlicht

IN SEARCH OF PEACE: The Story of Four Americans Who Won the Nobel Peace Prize

A FREE PEOPLE: The Story of the Declaration of Independence and The Men Who Wrote It

MARTIN LUTHER KING JR.: A Concise Biography

THEODORE ROOSEVELT: A Concise Biography

GANDHI: A Concise Biography

THE LEGENDS OF PAUL BUNYAN

ANDREWS' RAIDERS

THE DESPERATE ACT: The Assassination of Franz Ferdinand at Sarajevo

LET'S GO TO A WORLD'S FAIR

CONTENTS

Introduction: *The Dynamite King*	11
One: Theodore Roosevelt	
The Rough Rider	19
Speaking Softly	28
Two: Jane Addams	
"They Can Sit in the Dark"	37
Aunt Jane's Children	43
Three: Ralph Bunche	
A Small War	55
"Talking Is Better Than Shooting"	60
Four: Martin Luther King Jr.	
A New Weapon	73
"I Have a Dream"	80
Americans Who Have Won the Nobel Peace Prize	90
Some Suggestions for Further Reading	91
Index	92

IN SEARCH OF PEACE

The Story of Four Americans
Who Won the Nobel Peace Prize

Introduction: The Dynamite King

One day an inventor named Alfred Nobel read in the newspapers that he had died. Nobel knew this was an error, for he was very much alive. It was his brother who had died, and the newspapers had got the two men mixed up.

But Nobel was very upset. It was not the story of his death that was so disturbing, but what the newspapers wrote about him. They described him as a rich man who had made his fortune by inventing dynamite and other explosives. They called him "the dynamite king" and a "merchant of death."

This troubled Nobel, because he knew it was true. He was a genius who invented arms and explosives. He not only invented deadly weapons but manufactured and sold

Courtesy Wide World Photos

Introduction

them, which made him one of the richest men in the world.

Yet there was another side to Alfred Nobel. The inventor of dynamite wrote poetry and loved peace. He once called war "the horror of horrors and the greatest of all crimes." When he really died, he did not want to be remembered for what he had done for destruction and war. He wanted to be remembered for what he had done for humanity and peace.

Alfred Nobel was born on October 21, 1833, in Stockholm, Sweden. When he was nine years old, his family moved to Russia, where his father, Immanuel, was making explosives and weapons for the Tsar, the ruler of the Russian Empire.

Alfred had gone to school in Sweden for just one year and he never went again. In Russia, he and his two older brothers had a tutor. But before Alfred was seventeen, he gave up his studies to join his father's business.

One of the many things he soon learned was that people who make money from war do not like peace. When the Crimean War ended in 1856, Russia stopped ordering weapons from the Nobel family. Immanuel Nobel lost his fortune and returned to Sweden, where Alfred later joined him.

In Sweden, father and son experimented with explosives. Some years earlier, an Italian chemist had mixed nitric acid and glycerine. The result was nitroglycerine, a highly explosive liquid. It was very powerful but very unstable. Sometimes it blew up when it wasn't supposed to, and other times it didn't blow up at all.

The Nobels tried combining nitroglycerine with gunpowder to make shells for the Swedish army. It was Alfred who figured out the mixture that worked. Then he borrowed money and bought a house next to his parents' home. He turned it into a laboratory to experiment with nitroglycerine and to make explosives for sale.

Sometimes Alfred's younger brother, Oscar Emil, helped in the laboratory. One day in 1864, the building exploded with a roar. Alfred was not there at the time, but Oscar Emil was one of the four persons killed by the blast.

His brother's death did not stop Nobel's experiments. When Stockholm officials said he could no longer work in the city on something so dangerous, he moved his laboratory to a barge anchored in the middle of a lake. Although some people were frightened by Nobel's inventions, others saw how useful nitroglycerine could be for blasting away rock and soil, and building mines, roads, tunnels, and canals. Orders came in from all over the world.

But many of those who used nitroglycerine did not know how dangerous it was. A careless bounce or too much heat could cause a fearful explosion. There were many accidents, and a number of people died.

Nobel said it wasn't his fault if people were careless,

Introduction

but it really was. He was so eager to sell his new product that he hadn't bothered to make it safe first. Even one of his own nitroglycerine factories blew up. People began to call Nobel a murderer and a criminal, and some governments forbade the use of nitroglycerine.

Nobel was forced to find a way to make nitroglycerine safe or lose his business. He mixed it with a certain kind of earth called kieselguhr, which absorbed the nitroglycerine and made it stable so it would not explode until it was supposed to. The new product was called dynamite.

Dynamite made Nobel rich and famous, but it did not make him happy. He traveled, read, spoke five or six languages, and wrote poetry and plays, but he had few friends. Like many rich men, he was not sure whether people liked him or his money. He never married. Instead, he lived most of the time in a large, empty house in Paris, France, with his servants and his dreams.

For he did have dreams. He dreamed of a world where scientists would help men and not destroy them. He wanted to be such a scientist, but somehow he always came back to making explosives and weapons. "It is rather fiendish things we are working on," he told one of his assistants. He said that if a weapon was invented that was powerful enough to kill everyone at once, there would be no more war. But meanwhile he kept inventing and selling less powerful weapons, and wars continued.

IN SEARCH OF PEACE

The waste and horror of war upset many people besides Nobel. One of them was his friend Baroness Bertha von Suttner, who was active in an organization that wanted to set up an international court to settle quarrels between nations. Baroness von Suttner asked Nobel to give his fortune to the cause of peace. This was an idea that Nobel had been thinking of ever since the newspapers had printed the story of his death.

In 1893, he made a will which left part of his wealth to science and peace. In 1895, he wrote another will which went much further. A year later, on December 10, 1896, Alfred Nobel died.

Because of his second will, Nobel would be remembered not for what he did when he lived but for what he did when he died. Almost all of his huge fortune was to be used to set up five awards. These awards were to be given each year "to those persons who shall contribute most materially to benefitting mankind" in five areas—physics, chemistry, medicine, literature, and peace.

Since 1901, the Nobel Prizes have been awarded annually on December 10, the anniversary of Alfred Nobel's death. The winners receive money, a gold medal, and a diploma. In return, they are required to give a speech or lecture.

The Nobel Prize is one of the highest honors a man or woman can receive. The most important is the one that is

Introduction

given for peace. Some people do not care much about physics, chemistry, medicine, or good books, but the whole world cares about peace. The man or woman who helps bring peace to the world gives mankind its greatest gift.

Over the years, a number of Americans have won the Nobel Peace Prize. They were very different kinds of people, and they worked in very different ways. The chapters that follow tell the stories of four of these Americans. Taking separate paths, they all followed the road they hoped would lead to lasting peace.

Courtesy Harvard College Library

One

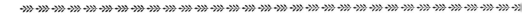

Theodore Roosevelt

The Rough Rider

The first American to win the Nobel Peace Prize was President Theodore Roosevelt. Some people thought this was an odd choice because, as a rule, Roosevelt thought war was dashing and heroic. "This country needs a war," he said more than once.

Roosevelt believed there were two kinds of war, just and unjust. "Unjust war is dreadful," he wrote, "a just war may be the highest duty." But it is often hard to agree on what a just war is. For Roosevelt, any war that he wanted to be in was just. Many boys dream of being war heroes, but Roosevelt's dream never died, not even when he was an old

Courtesy
Theodore Roosevelt Association

Teedie at the age of ten.

man. Perhaps this was because he had been a small, sickly boy who was always being threatened by bigger bullies.

Roosevelt was born in New York City on October 27, 1858. His nickname was Teedie, not Teddy. He hated to be called Teddy, especially after he grew up.

Although Teedie was often ill, he was very bright and he loved to study nature and animals. One day, when he was on his way to the market to buy strawberries, he saw a dead seal. He got the seal's skull and used it to start a museum of natural history. His collection included some dead mice which he kept in a bureau drawer. His mother told a maid to clean them out, and Teedie said it was a "loss to science."

Teedie went to a private school for a while, but most of

his early education came from a tutor, two trips to Europe with his family, and reading books. When he was eighteen, Theodore Roosevelt entered Harvard College. While he was a student, he met a very pretty seventeen-year-old girl named Alice Lee and fell in love at once. They were married on his twenty-second birthday.

By then Roosevelt had graduated from college. He had also become interested in politics and joined the Republican Party. In the fall of 1881, he was elected to the New York state legislature, where he served three terms.

The legislature met in Albany, in upstate New York. On February 13, 1884, Roosevelt received a telegram from his home in Manhattan. Alice had given birth to a baby girl. As Roosevelt got ready to leave Albany, he received a second telegram which said that Alice was ill.

It was almost midnight when Roosevelt got home. His brother met him at the door. "There is a curse on this house!" he said. "Mother is dying and Alice is dying too."

At about three in the morning, Roosevelt's mother died of typhoid fever. Less than twelve hours later, his wife died of a kidney disease. She was twenty-two years old.

Roosevelt was so torn by grief he did not know what to do. A few months later, he made up his mind. He asked one of his sisters to care for his baby daughter, then he headed West. Someone said he "hiked away to the wilderness to get away from the world."

Roosevelt became a first-rate boxer at Harvard.
Courtesy Theodore Roosevelt Association

Theodore Roosevelt

Roosevelt went to the Badlands, in what is now North Dakota. He had been there before, and he already owned a cattle ranch. Now he bought a second ranch and stayed out West for two years enjoying adventures most boys only imagine. He knocked out a drunken cowboy who was holding two guns to his head. He spent forty hours in the saddle rounding up stampeding cattle. He shot a grizzly bear between the eyes. He even captured thieves who had stolen his boat and brought them to jail.

In 1886, Roosevelt returned to New York City, where he ran for mayor and lost. A few weeks later he married a childhood friend, Edith Kermit Carow. They moved to Sagamore Hill, a house he had built at Oyster Bay, Long Island.

At different times during the next ten years, Roosevelt wrote books, worked for the government, and ran the New York City police department. To be sure the police were doing their duty, Roosevelt walked the streets at night disguised in a black cape with a hat pulled low over his eyes. Once, when he saw a policeman taking time out for a beer, he chased him down the street and caught him.

In 1897, President William McKinley appointed Roosevelt Assistant Secretary of the Navy. At that time, Cuba was in revolt against Spain, which ruled the island. Roosevelt wanted to help the Cubans because he thought Spain should be driven out of the Western Hemisphere.

IN SEARCH OF PEACE

America declared war on Spain in April, 1898, and Roosevelt volunteered for active duty. He was made lieutenant-colonel of a cavalry regiment. The commander was a regular army surgeon, Colonel Leonard Wood, but the men were volunteers. They included cowboys, Indians, outlaws, and Harvard students. Because they were wild and hard to control, the press called them the Rough Riders.

While the Rough Riders trained in Texas, Roosevelt fretted for fear the war might be over before he got to Cuba.

Police Commissioner Roosevelt in his office at Police Headquarters.
Courtesy Theodore Roosevelt Association

Theodore Roosevelt

"It will be awful if we miss the fun," he wrote. The regiment finally sailed in June. Although the men were trained as cavalry, their horses were left behind. Only the officers' horses were shipped.

Colonel Wood was so eager for action that he marched the Rough Riders into ambush on June 24. Roosevelt led his men on foot, and his sword kept tripping him by catching between his legs. He decided never again to use it in battle.

A few days after the ambush, in which sixteen Americans were killed, Colonel Wood was promoted, and Roosevelt took full command of the Rough Riders. On June 30, the American forces, including Roosevelt's regiment, received orders to attack the Spanish stronghold at Santiago.

The American assault began at dawn on July 1. Within minutes, the Rough Riders were caught in a hail of Spanish fire, and Roosevelt's wrist was lightly bruised by shrapnel. He led his men forward through high grass and heavy shelling, then waited for orders. While he waited, men died on all sides of him.

Orders finally came to move forward and support the soldiers who were attacking the Spaniards on the hills in front of them. Roosevelt jumped onto his horse and at that moment began what he called his "crowded hour."

After marching his men forward, Roosevelt found the captain of the soldiers, who were firing from the foot of the hills. Roosevelt told him the only way to take the hills was to rush them. The officer said he could not charge without orders. Roosevelt asked where his colonel was, but he was not in sight.

"Then I am the ranking officer here," said Roosevelt, "and I give the order to charge."

The captain hesitated. "Then let my men through, sir," snapped Roosevelt. Waving his hat, Roosevelt gave the order to charge the hill at his right, which was later called Kettle Hill. "I galloped toward the hill," he later wrote, "passing the shouting, cheering, firing men, and went up the lane, splashing through a small stream. When I got abreast of the ranch buildings on the top of Kettle Hill, I turned and went up the slope. Being on horseback, I was, of course, able to get ahead of the men on foot."

Roosevelt's charge up Kettle Hill made him a national hero. He called it "great fun" and said his part in the war gave him "pride and satisfaction." He remembered the heroics and the glory more than he remembered the dead and the wounded. He often forgot that more Americans were killed by yellow fever and malaria than by the Spaniards, and that many people thought the Spanish-American War was unnecessary and unjust.

The famous charge led Roosevelt not only to the top of the hill but to the White House as well. He was still in Cuba when Republican leaders chose him to run for governor of New York State. Roosevelt won the campaign. Just two

Courtesy Theodore Roosevelt Association

Colonel Roosevelt and some of his Rough Riders.

years later, he became Vice President when President McKinley was elected to a second term. Roosevelt planned to run for President in 1904, but on September 6, 1901, an assassin shot McKinley at a fair in Buffalo, New York.

At first, the President's doctors thought he would live. To let the country know all was well, Vice President Roosevelt and his family went climbing in the Adirondack Mountains in upstate New York. On September 13, a guide brought Roosevelt a message which said, "The President appears to be dying."

Late that night, Roosevelt received a second message telling him to go to North Creek station, where a special train would take him to Buffalo. The station was thirty-five miles from Roosevelt's mountain camp, and the roads had been washed out by rainstorms. In a horse-drawn buckboard wagon, Roosevelt and a driver plunged through the blackness. If the horses had stumbled, Roosevelt would have been pitched over the side of the mountain to his death.

It was dawn by the time he reached the station. There he learned that McKinley had died during the night. The special train brought Roosevelt to Buffalo, where he took the oath of President. It was September 14, 1901, six weeks before his forty-third birthday.

Speaking Softly

In some ways, Roosevelt was one of the best Presidents

Theodore Roosevelt

America ever had. He took office at a time when the country was run by big business, and he used his powers to curb corporations that got too large. He also fought for the rights of the worker. When 140,000 coal miners struck for higher wages, shorter hours, and decent working conditions, Roosevelt forced the mine owners to agree to a fair settlement.

Although Roosevelt didn't always get what he wanted, he supported regulation of the railroads, a pure food and drug act, laws that would abolish child labor, and other major reforms. This made him very popular. When he ran for his own term as President in 1904, he won easily.

Roosevelt was America's first modern President. He was vigorous and active; everything interested him and

T.R. timing the races around the barn at Sagamore Hill.

Courtesy Theodore Roosevelt Association

everything he did interested the public. He blew the stuffiness out of the White House by having pillow fights with his children before state dinners. He loved sports and went hiking, hunting, and picnicking every chance he had.

Because he loved nature, he did everything he could to preserve it. He protected forests from greedy men who wanted to chop down the trees for lumber. He created five national parks so Americans could see how beautiful their country is. He also created many wildlife preserves where animals would be safe from hunters.

One of Roosevelt's favorite proverbs was "Speak softly and carry a big stick; you will go far." That meant, don't argue too much, but be well armed for a fight if one comes. When he first became President, Roosevelt was always ready for a fight. If America disagreed with another country, even over a minor issue, he would threaten to use troops.

After he decided a canal should be built across Panama, he let nothing stop him. Panama then belonged to Colombia, which did not like the terms America offered. Instead of offering better terms, Roosevelt sent American ships and marines to Panama. He later boasted, "I took Panama," and called it "the most important action I took in foreign affairs." He was so sure the canal was right for America that he did not care whether it was right for Panama.

But Roosevelt was not always so thoughtless of other nations. He understood that war could be wasteful and

Inspecting the Panama Canal.
Courtesy Harvard College Library

IN SEARCH OF PEACE

pointless, and he believed that an international court could help settle quarrels between nations. In 1899, a world court was set up at The Hague, a city in Holland. But no nation would use the world court for fear that other nations would think it a sign of weakness.

It was Theodore Roosevelt who gave the Hague court its first case, a dispute between the United States and Mexico. Once Roosevelt had used the court, statesmen of other nations followed his lead. Many other cases were given to the court to settle.

Roosevelt not only helped make The Hague a useful place to settle disputes, but he ended one major war himself. This was a war between Russia and Japan.

One of the things Roosevelt believed in was a balance of power. He didn't think any one nation should be so big and powerful that it threatened world peace. He felt that in Asia there was a good balance of power between Russia and Japan. Each kept the other from becoming too strong.

But neither Russia nor Japan was satisfied with what it had. Both nations wanted to expand, and both wanted the same territory. On February 8, 1904, Japan attacked the Russian fleet without warning.

At first Roosevelt was pleased, because he had begun to think the Russians were getting too powerful. "I think the Japanese will whip them handsomely," he said. Since Russia was huge and Japan was tiny, Roosevelt cheered for the underdog. He even thought of using the American fleet to help the Japanese.

But the Japanese didn't need any help. They beat the Russians so badly that Roosevelt began to fear Japan, not Russia, would upset the balance of power in Asia. He also feared the Japanese would become "puffed up with pride and turn against us."

By the beginning of 1905, Roosevelt had decided the Russo-Japanese War must end. He offered to act as mediator, someone who listens to both sides and suggests a fair settlement. Both nations accepted his offer. But it is easier to get into a war than to get out of it, and there were many problems arranging the details of a peace conference. "I have been growing nearly mad in the effort to get Russia and Japan together," Roosevelt told a friend.

The peace conference was finally held at Portsmouth, New Hampshire, in August, 1905. By the end of the month, it looked as if it would fail. Japan wanted the island of Sakhalin, off Siberia, as well as an indemnity, or large payment of money, from Russia. Russia refused both demands.

Roosevelt advised Russia to give the Japanese the southern part of Sakhalin, because they already held it anyway. Then he advised the Japanese to settle for half of Sakhalin and forget about the indemnity, because Russia was too big to conquer and Japan could not afford to fight forever. Both sides agreed and peace terms were reached on August 30.

IN SEARCH OF PEACE

"I believe that what I did was for the best interests of both [Russia and Japan] and of the world at large," wrote Roosevelt. Others thought so too, and for ending the Russo-Japanese War, Roosevelt was awarded the Nobel Peace Prize in 1906.

Two years later, Roosevelt left the White House. He could probably have been elected President again, but he thought two terms were enough. He went off to Africa to hunt wild game. By the time he returned to America a year later, he was so unhappy with the new President, William Howard Taft, that he decided to run for President again in 1912.

Roosevelt lost the Republican nomination to Taft, so he ran as a candidate of the Progressive Party, a national reform movement. During the campaign, a madman shot him in the chest. A rolled-up speech and an eyeglass case in his pocket helped stop the bullet and save his life.

The election was won by the Democratic candidate, Woodrow Wilson.

Always seeking new adventures, Roosevelt headed south to Brazil to explore an unmapped river. He almost died in the jungle of fever and disease, but he said he had to make the trip because "it was my last chance to be a boy."

When World War I began in 1914, Roosevelt forgot how useful a peacemaker could be and remembered only how much fun it had been to charge up Kettle Hill. He called President Wilson a "coward" for trying to keep the

Theodore Roosevelt

United States out of the war. He tried to get the Republican nomination to run against Wilson in 1916, but the Republicans refused to nominate him. Wilson was reelected.

The United States finally did enter the war in April, 1917. Roosevelt volunteered to lead a division, even though he was fifty-nine years old, half-blind, half-deaf, and often ill. His request was denied. But his four sons went to war, and the youngest was killed.

Although he was old and ill, Roosevelt never lost the urge to return to the White House. By the summer of 1918 he was making plans to run for President in 1920. But he never had the chance. Early in the morning of January 6, 1919, he died in his sleep.

Long after his death, Roosevelt is remembered as a President who was a reformer at home but warlike in his foreign policy. It is often forgotten that once, when it was very important, Roosevelt was also a man of peace.

Courtesy
Theodore Roosevelt Association

Russo-Japanese peace delegates with T.R.

Courtesy Hull House Association

Two

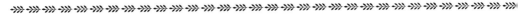

Jane Addams

"They Can Sit in the Dark"

No two people could have been more different than the first American man and the first American woman who won the Nobel Peace Prize. Theodore Roosevelt thought that many wars were just, but Jane Addams was a pacifist. She believed all wars were bad. "Wars are not waged for honor, or for understanding, but for destruction," she said.

    Roosevelt and Jane Addams lived at about the same time, and their paths often crossed. They both agreed that every man should have the right to a decent job, that women should be able to vote, and that children belong in schools rather than in factories.

IN SEARCH OF PEACE

But Jane Addams was certain there could be no progress in a world at war. To fight poverty, injustice, and hunger, there had to be peace. War created hate, killed men, starved women and children, and destroyed cities. When the war was over, the old problems remained. Since Roosevelt thought war could be fun, pacifists like Jane Addams made him mad. "Jane Addams—don't talk to me about Jane Addams!" he once snapped. "She is all wrong about peace. But she is a fine woman in every other way."

Jane Addams was a very fine woman. For her, no victory in battle was as glorious as cleaning up a slum or building a playground. She believed that the terrible problem of war and peace would be settled when every man had a decent life. She believed that no man could be comfortable until every man was cared for.

Jane Addams could have been comfortable all of her life, if she had wanted to be. She was born on September 6, 1860, in Cedarville, Illinois. Her mother died when she was only two years old. Her father was a wealthy businessman and a member of the Illinois state legislature. One of his friends was President Abraham Lincoln. When Lincoln was shot, Jane saw her father cry. For the first time in her life, she understood that grownups weep too.

Mr. Addams was a rather stern man. One day Jane told a lie. When she went to bed that night she found she could not sleep. Although she dreaded the dark, she slipped

Courtesy Hull House Association
Jane Addams as a little girl.

through the house to her father's room and told him what she had done. All he said was that if he had a little girl who told lies, he was very glad she felt too bad to go to sleep afterward.

Jane was six years old when she first saw poverty as she rode with her father through the poor section of a nearby town. She told him that when she grew up she wanted to live in a big house "right in the midst of horrid little houses like these." Another time, her father told her to wear her old cloak to church instead of her pretty new one so she would not make the poorer girls feel bad. Jane found herself thinking about the difference between being rich and poor, and wondering what could be done about it.

When Jane was eight, her father married again. Her new stepbrother, George, was just a few months younger

Courtesy Jane Addams' Memorial Collection
University of Illinois, Chicago Circle

From left to right: Jane Addams, her stepmother Anna Holdeman Addams, and her stepbrother George Holdeman.

than she was, and he became her closest friend. Together they went to school and afterward played their favorite game of Crusades. With a green feather in his hat and a green wooden sword, George liked to pretend he was the Knight of the Green Plume.

The childhood games ended when Jane and George went off to different colleges. Jane went to Rockford Seminary and graduated at the head of her class. George wanted to marry her, and so did other young men, but she refused them. She studied medicine for a few months and then decided she didn't want to be a doctor. Her father had died and left her some property, so she did not have to work. Yet she wanted to do something, though she couldn't decide what it should be.

She became ill and spent many months in bed. A doctor suggested a trip to Europe would be good for her. She went abroad, but returned more troubled than ever. She had seen how terrible it was to be poor. In Ireland she found people living in windowless huts. Someone told her that it didn't matter, "they can sit in the dark."

In London she went to an outdoor market where thousands of poor people bought the rotting fruits and vegetables that were all they could afford. As she later wrote, she watched in horror as one man who had bought a cabbage "instantly sat down on the curb, tore it with his teeth, and hastily devoured it, unwashed and uncooked as it was."

When Jane Addams was twenty-seven, she made a second trip to Europe. With four friends she went to a bullfight in Madrid. The other women could not bear the brutality and left early, but Jane Addams stayed. Afterward, she felt guilty, not only about that afternoon but about her whole life. She had watched five bulls slaughtered and had done nothing, and she had seen poverty and suffering and had done nothing. She decided she was fooling herself by thinking she was still preparing for her life's work. The time to begin her life's work was now.

The next day she told her friend Ellen Gates Starr that

Courtesy Jane Addams' Memorial Collection
University of Illinois, Chicago Circle

Jane Addams, holding a parasol, with some of her Rockford Seminary classmates.

she was ready to live in a big house "in the midst of horrid little houses." She left her friends and went to London to visit a place called Toynbee Hall.

Toynbee Hall was the first settlement house in the world. A settlement house is a place in a crowded city where people who are usually richer and better-educated "settle" to help the poor people in the neighborhood. The men who founded Toynbee Hall believed that the poor needed more than food and charity. In clubs and classes at Toynbee Hall, the poor people of London could enjoy books, music, art, and sports. It was also a place where they could meet and enjoy each other's company.

Jane Addams studied Toynbee Hall, as well as other places and programs that helped the poor. By the time she returned to America, she was no longer looking for something to do with her life. She had found it.

Aunt Jane's Children

Jane Addams decided to open a settlement house in Chicago, Illinois. Chicago was the second largest city in America, and three quarters of the people there were immigrants. They were Italians, Irish, Germans, Czechs, and others who had come to America to seek a better life. Many of them had not found it.

Families crowded into little wooden houses without

Courtesy Jane Addams' Memorial Collection
University of Illinois, Chicago Circle

Ellen Gates Starr (at left) serves tea to a neighborhood boy and to Jane Addams.

water or plumbing. There were not enough schools for the children and not enough jobs for the adults. Men who were lucky might earn $2.50 for a twelve-hour day. Children who were forced to work to help their parents survive earned as little as four cents an hour.

Jane Addams found a large house on South Halsted Street, in the midst of all the misery. It had once belonged to a rich man named Charles J. Hull, and his cousin gave it to Jane Addams free.

Jane Addams and Ellen Gates Starr moved into Hull House in September, 1889. At first the people in the neighborhood were suspicious, but they soon found the two women were warm, friendly, and helpful. Other men and women moved into Hull House to help. Before long the settlement house was serving thousands of people.

In the morning there was a kindergarten for small children. In the afternoon there were clubs and classes for teen-agers. The girls learned how to sew, and the boys played checkers or put on plays.

In the evening there were classes for adults. They could learn to read and write English or enjoy their favorite games or sports. Or they could just come to Hull House for friendship or advice.

Jane Addams, some children and staff of Hull House, 1931. They are looking at a portrait of Jennie Dow who organized the first kindergarten at Hull House in 1889.

Courtesy Chicago Historical Society

There was a reading room at Hull House, as well as a gymnasium and a coffee shop. The people of the neighborhood often held dances or weddings in the gym. The coffee shop became a place for everyone to gather and chat.

Working in the slums of Chicago, Jane Addams learned a lot about poverty that she had never known before. At a Christmas party at Hull House, she was surprised when the children would not eat candy. Then she discovered they had been working fourteen hours a day in a candy factory. The sight of it made them sick.

Jane Addams realized the poor needed justice rather than charity. She began to fight for laws against child labor. Factory owners became angry. They wanted children to work because they paid them so little. These men threatened and insulted Jane Addams. One of them offered her $50,000 to stop fighting for a child labor law. But she refused. In 1903, fourteen years after that first Christmas party at Hull House, a child labor law was finally passed in Illinois.

Jane Addams became involved in many crusades. She fought for higher wages and better working conditions for adults. She supported labor unions so workers could fight together for a better life. She was one of the founders of the National Association for the Advancement of Colored People (NAACP).

She not only got others to work for good causes, but worked for them herself. Because garbage breeds disease,

Courtesy Jane Addams' Memorial Collection
University of Illinois, Chicago Circle

From 1910 on, Hull House looked like this.

she became garbage inspector for her district. She rose at six every morning to be sure the garbage collectors were doing their work.

Her greatest love was children. One day a wealthy young man who owned some old houses near Hull House heard her make a speech about helping other people. He went to her and asked what he could do.

"You might tear the buildings down and make the lots a place for the children to play on," she said. "They have nothing but the streets now."

"Do as you please about that," he replied.

"Will you pay for tearing them down?" she asked.

"I don't see why I should," he replied.

"And will you pay the taxes?" she continued.

Now he was angry. "You ask too much," he said, and went away. But as the man wrote afterward, Jane Addams "was the first person who ever forced me to try to think things out. You might say she . . . civilized me."

A week later he returned and said, "I'll do whatever you say." The buildings were torn down and the lots were turned into Chicago's first public playground.

By 1910, Jane Addams was so well known for her good works that she was one of the most famous women in America. Her world went far beyond Hull House, as she struggled for a better life not only for the people of Chicago but throughout the nation. She made speeches, wrote articles and books, and helped found many organizations. She was called on to settle labor disputes and served on Chicago's Board of Education for several years. Anyone who needed help could come to her, for she was both kind and fearless.

Twice, burglars crept into her room at Hull House while she slept. The first time she asked the burglar to be quiet because her nephew was sleeping in the next room. When the startled thief tried to escape through the window, she said, "You'll be hurt if you go out that way. Go down by the stairs and let yourself out."

She had a long chat with the second burglar and discovered that he needed a job. She told him to come back the next day, and she helped him find one.

In 1912, when Theodore Roosevelt decided to run for

Jane Addams

President as a candidate of the Progressive Party, he asked Jane Addams for help. She seconded his nomination and got almost as much applause as he did. Her support was said to be worth a million votes. Even though she disagreed with Roosevelt's ideas about war, she backed him because the Progressive Party program on which he ran called for many reforms. She campaigned across the country for the reforms, not for Roosevelt. And even though Roosevelt lost his campaign, Jane Addams won hers. Many of the laws she wanted were passed under the new President, Woodrow Wilson.

Two years after the Progressive Party campaign, Jane Addams became involved in another campaign, the hardest and most important of her life. When World War I began in August, 1914, she opposed it as she opposed all wars. She believed that every life was sacred, and she said she couldn't see how you could help people by killing them.

Her greatest objection to war was that it made progress impossible. Men could not build a better world while they were killing each other. She knew that many people found war glorious, and she wished people could be as excited by peace as they are by war. "When once we surround human life with the same kind of heroism and admiration that we have surrounded war," she said, "we can say that . . . war will become impossible."

Pacifists in Europe and America organized to oppose

Jane Addams (at right) with Mary Eliza McDowell in 1917.
Courtesy Chicago Historical Society

Jane Addams

the war, and Jane Addams became one of the founders of the Women's International League for Peace and Freedom. The League asked the neutral nations—those countries that were not at war—to offer continuous mediation to those that were.

Theodore Roosevelt called the women "cowards" and said their plan was "silly." But when Jane Addams and other delegates visited the heads of the various warring governments, they found most of them eager to end the fighting. What they needed was someone to help them find an honorable way out. Jane Addams also found that the neutral nations would be happy to mediate if the United States took the lead.

But President Wilson rejected her advice. He had his own plans for mediation, which failed. America entered the war in April, 1917. Until then there were many American pacifists, but once their country was at war, most of them felt they should support it. Jane Addams loved America too, but she thought war was the wrong way to solve problems. "Reason and good will can settle any difficulty between any set of men," she insisted, "whether they be groups of men or groups of nations."

But no one would listen to her now. Many of her friends turned against her. She was called Communist, traitor, un-American. She discovered it was dangerous and unpopular to be for peace in wartime. "You know," she said sadly, "I am really getting old. I find it is not as easy to love my enemies as it used to be."

Courtesy Hull House Association

Miss Addams visits Japan in 1923 on behalf of the Women's International League for Peace and Freedom.

By the time the war ended in 1918, Jane Addams had decided there would be world peace only if poverty, ignorance, disease, and injustice were wiped out everywhere. In 1931, her tireless work was rewarded with the Nobel Peace Prize, which she shared with another American, Nicholas Murray Butler, an educator and statesman.

By now all of the insults and anger had been forgotten. She was once again an important public figure. In May, 1935, a dinner was given in her honor in Washington, D.C.

Jane Addams

After all of the great and famous people had praised her, Jane Addams spoke.

"We don't expect to change human nature, we people of peace," she said, "but we do expect to change human behavior." Then she added, "The worst thing about war is not the poison gas which wipes out lives and destroys cities, but the poison it spreads in the minds of man."

Less than three weeks later, on May 21, 1935, Jane Addams died. Her funeral was at Hull House, so the thousands of people she had helped could say good-by. Her six-year-old grandniece looked at the huge crowd of mourners and asked, "Are we all Aunt Jane's children?"

Many words of honor and praise were spoken of Jane Addams both before and after her death. Perhaps the truest came from an Englishman who called her "the only saint America had produced."

Courtesy United Nations

Three

Ralph Bunche

A Small War

When two people quarrel, they often need a third person to help them settle their dispute. It is the same with nations. When two countries go to war, it is often necessary for an outsider to act as mediator. The mediator tries to make both sides compromise—or give in a little—until they can find common ground for making peace.

A mediator can be just one man; Theodore Roosevelt was the mediator who settled the Russo-Japanese War. A nation or group of nations can also act as mediator; Jane Addams wanted the neutral countries to settle World War I. Finally, the mediator can be a world organization; an organization that is more important than any single country because it represents all the countries of the world.

The idea of a world organization to keep the peace goes far back into history, but it has never worked. After the horror and destruction of World War II, however, the United Nations was founded in 1945 to provide peace with justice for all mankind. But within two years, it was faced with a major challenge, as fighting erupted in the Middle East. If the United Nations could not make peace, it would be worthless.

International organizations, like nations, are only as good as the men who serve them. In this Middle Eastern crisis, the United Nations would eventually turn to an American named Ralph Bunche.

Ralph Johnson Bunche was born in Detroit, Michigan, on August 7, 1904. His maternal grandfather, Thomas Nelson Johnson, was a schoolteacher and principal.

When Mr. Johnson died, he left a wife, Lucy, and five children. The Johnson family was close, and even after one of the daughters, Olive, married a barber named Fred Bunche, they all lived together. Ralph Bunche grew up in the midst of what he calls a "clan" rather than a family. At the head of the clan was his tiny, soft-spoken grandmother, whom he called Nana.

Ralph Bunche still remembers Nana's prune pies and apple dumplings, and her golden fried chicken. He also re-

Ralph Bunche

members her fierce pride, and how often she reminded the family that they were as good as anybody on earth, and that character and decency mattered more than money or the color of their skin, which was black.

The Johnson clan was "poor but merry," according to Dr. Bunche. Most of the family worked, including Ralph, who was a newsboy. They loved music, and all five of the Johnson children played instruments. Together they made up a small performing company that sang and put on one-act plays. Ralph sometimes had a walk-on part, but he had to keep his mouth closed. "For the sake of our good name," Nana told him one day, "never let anybody hear you sing."

Although they were black, the Johnsons did not suffer much from discrimination, for there were not many Negroes in Detroit then, and there was no ghetto. Ralph's playmates were white, and the first discrimination he saw was not against blacks but against Italians, who were America's newest group of immigrants.

As a boy, Ralph was lively and mischievous. Once he smoked one of his father's cigars. He became so ill that Nana would not let anyone punish him because she felt he had been punished enough.

When Ralph was about seven years old, the Johnson clan made the first of several moves to different cities, to try to find a better climate for his mother, who was ill. He was ten when they settled in Albuquerque, New Mexico. There he saw his first Indian and learned to ride pinto ponies bareback. Sometimes he and his father went hunting and brought back quail and rabbits for dinner.

But Ralph's pleasant stay in the Southwest ended in tragedy. His mother and father died within three months of each other, and at the age of thirteen Ralph Bunche was an orphan. But he was not alone, for he still had his Nana and the rest of the Johnson clan, as well as a younger sister.

In 1917, the clan moved to Los Angeles. Life was hard sometimes, but no matter what happened, Nana had made up her mind about one thing. Ralph was not going to drop out of school. He was going to get an education and be somebody someday.

To earn money while he was in school, Ralph worked as a newsboy again. He had one of his first bitter tastes of color discrimination when he and a friend went to a newsboys' picnic and were not allowed to use a swimming pool because they were black.

In high school, Ralph was not only a top student but a top athlete, winning letters in baseball, football, and basketball. He graduated with honors, and the University of California in Los Angeles gave him a scholarship. Although he didn't have to pay for his classes, he needed money to live on. He supported himself by running a cleaning service for some small stores and offices.

Again he graduated with honors, and Harvard Univer-

Ralph Bunche

sity offered him a scholarship to study for a master's degree. But he didn't have the money to travel from California to Massachusetts. A group of Negro women started a collection and raised $1,000 "to send our Ralph to Harvard."

After winning his master's degree, Ralph Bunche taught at Howard, a Negro university in Washington, D.C. He married one of his students, and received a doctor's degree from Harvard. He also traveled in Europe, Africa, and Asia studying the dark-skinned people of the world.

In time, Dr. Bunche became an expert on race, race relations, and colonial people. Colonial people are those who have no real government of their own. They are ruled by another nation.

During World War II, Dr. Bunche did intelligence work for the government. In 1944 he became the first Negro to be given an important job with the State Department.

After the war, Dr. Bunche worked for the United Nations. In the spring of 1947, he was asked to join a United Nations commission investigating the situation in Palestine. Although Dr. Bunche's specialty was Africa and Asia, not the Middle East, he agreed to go, for Palestine was one of the most troubled areas in the world.

Jews driven out of Europe during World War II claimed Palestine as the land of their fathers and wanted to make it their homeland. But the Arabs, who had lived there for over 1,300 years, said it belonged to them. Bloody fight-

IN SEARCH OF PEACE

ing broke out, and the British, who had ruled Palestine since World War I, asked the United Nations for help.

The United Nations commission decided that Palestine should be divided into two separate states, one for the Jews and one for the Arabs. The Jews accepted this plan but the Arabs would not.

At midnight on May 14, 1948, the British officially withdrew from Palestine. That afternoon the Jews proclaimed the birth of the state of Israel. The Arab nations that surrounded the new state attacked on three sides. War was raging in the Middle East, and there was fear it might spread to Europe. Besides, if the United Nations could do nothing about a small war, how could it do anything about a large one? The United Nations had to make peace in Palestine or it might not survive.

"Talking Is Better Than Shooting"

The United Nations chose Count Folke Bernadotte, a Swedish diplomat, as official mediator. As Count Bernadotte's top aide, Dr. Ralph Bunche was asked to introduce the mediator to Palestine and its problems. The first time they met was at an airport in Paris. Count Bernadotte briskly shook Dr. Bunche's hand, bowed, and said, "Tell me, what do they want me to do out there in Palestine?"

"They just want you to go out there and stop the fighting, that's all," said Dr. Bunche.

Ralph Bunche

"With what?" asked the Count.

"With your bare hands," replied Dr. Bunche.

"All right," said Count Bernadotte, "we'll go."

One of the many problems Count Bernadotte had to face was that some men on both sides did not want the United Nations to make peace. These men wanted the war fought to the bitter end, with the winner taking all. The United Nations cars in which Count Bernadotte and Dr. Bunche rode were sometimes fired upon by snipers.

Count Bernadotte decided to establish his headquarters in a neutral place and chose the Greek island of Rhodes. The United Nations ordered a cease-fire in Palestine, but both sides often ignored it. Meanwhile, Count Bernadotte prepared a plan for a permanent peace settlement which he

Count Bernadotte, with Dr. Bunche to his left, holds a press conference.

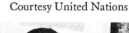

Courtesy United Nations

wanted to recommend to the United Nations.

On September 17, Count Bernadotte flew to Jerusalem, in Palestine, to check a site for the truce talks which he hoped to hold there. Dr. Bunche stayed behind in Rhodes to finish the report for the United Nations. He was to meet Count Bernadotte in Jerusalem at three o'clock in the afternoon so they could inspect the site together.

Because Count Bernadotte was always on time, Dr. Bunche tried never to be late. But his plane was delayed in Lebanon with a damaged wheel. When he finally landed in Jerusalem, there was another unexpected delay. The airport was behind Arab lines. When Dr. Bunche attempted to cross into Israeli territory in a jeep, he was stopped at the Israeli line. The officer on duty had left and a corporal was in charge. Because the corporal did not know Dr. Bunche and did not understand English, he would not let him through.

Meanwhile Count Bernadotte, who never waited for anyone, decided to wait for Dr. Bunche. While he waited, a French officer, Colonel Andre Serot, came up and introduced himself. During World War II, Count Bernadotte, as head of the Swedish Red Cross, had helped free many prisoners from German concentration camps. One of those freed was Serot's wife, and the colonel wanted to thank him.

After waiting for Dr. Bunche for about twenty minutes, Count Bernadotte decided to go on without him. He invited Colonel Serot to take Dr. Bunche's place in his car, and the colonel accepted.

At about five o'clock that afternoon, the three-car convoy was halted by several men in a jeep. The United Nations officials thought this was a routine checkpoint. No one was alarmed when two armed men walked calmly down the line of cars, peering into each one.

But the men were Israeli terrorists, who had sworn to kill both Count Bernadotte and Dr. Bunche. When they recognized the Count, who was sitting in the rear of the third car, one of the men pushed his gun through the window and fired. The first bullet struck Colonel Serot in the temple, killing him instantly. Then Count Bernadotte was shot in the chest fifteen times.

Dr. Bunche was still being held at the Israeli line when an Israeli officer drove up and told him Count Bernadotte had been shot. Dr. Bunche was quickly driven to the United Nations headquarters in Jerusalem. He was there when the two bodies were carried in.

After Count Bernadotte's assassination, the United Nations asked Dr. Bunche to take over as acting mediator. Even though he had so narrowly escaped death, he agreed.

Talks began on Rhodes in January, 1949. The first negotiations involved the Israelis and the Egyptians. Dr. Bunche worked sixteen to twenty hours a day, talking first to one side, then the other. One of his favorite phrases was,

Courtesy United Nations

The United Nations acting mediator, Dr. Ralph Bunche, signs the General Armistice Agreement between the Egyptian and Israeli governments.

"Talking is better than shooting," and he used it often. Even though there was arguing over the smallest details, his secretary said, "I never once saw him lose his temper. Whenever the tension became too great, he'd knock off for a game of ping-pong or billiards."

Israel and Egypt signed an armistice agreement on February 24. The second armistice, between Israel and Jordan, was signed on April 3. While the talks with Egypt and Jordan were held on Rhodes, the United Nations also arranged for talks with Lebanon and Syria in the war zone. Lebanon signed a treaty with Israel on March 23, and Syria signed on July 20. The war was over.

Ralph Bunche

As the talks ended on Rhodes, Dr. Bunche presented each of the delegates with a piece of pottery he had ordered earlier and had inscribed. The head of the Israeli delegation, who saw the pottery before the truces were arranged, asked Dr. Bunche what he would do with it if the conferences failed. "I'll break it over your heads," he replied.

When Dr. Bunche returned to America, he was greeted as a hero, for not only had he brought peace to Palestine, but many people felt he had saved the United Nations. There were awards, medals, and speeches, a ticker tape parade in New York, and a Ralph Bunche Day in Los Angeles. President Harry S Truman asked him to become an Assistant Secretary of State, which was then the highest government position ever offered a Negro. But Dr. Bunche refused because he would have had to live in Washington, which was a segregated city. He remembered that when he lived there earlier, his children could not go to the neighborhood school because it was for whites only. "I prefer to live as a free man," he told the President. "I agree with you," President Truman replied.

Dr. Bunche decided to live in New York City and continue to work for the United Nations. One day in September, 1950, as he was finishing his lunch, his secretary rushed up to him and said, "I have a surprise for you. You've won the Nobel Peace Prize."

Dr. Bunche was the first Negro to win the Peace Prize,

Courtesy Wide World Photos

Dr. Ralph Bunche reads his Nobel Peace Prize diploma just after it was handed to him during a ceremony in Oslo University dining hall.

but he wasn't thinking of his color when he heard about the award. He was thinking of Count Bernadotte and everyone else, living and dead, who had helped bring about the Palestinian peace. He knew he had not succeeded only because he was Ralph Bunche, but because he was a representative of the United Nations. "I more than anyone recognize the extent to which my peace efforts flowed from the strength of the United Nations," he said. "I was in Palestine as an official of the United Nations."

Dr. Bunche had expected the armistice in Palestine to last only two or three years, and he hoped a more permanent settlement would soon be arranged. But nothing further was done, and serious clashes later broke out in the area, because the problems that caused the war have not been solved.

Because of the United Nations, however, the clashes have not yet turned into a long or major war. The world organization is still trying to find solutions both Israelis and Arabs will accept.

The truce that Dr. Bunche arranged not only lasted much longer than he expected, but it came at a time when the United Nations had to prove it could work. Because it worked, people gained faith in the organization, and it became stronger in dealing with other issues. The United Nations has since settled many disputes and prevented small wars from becoming large ones. Through its many agencies, it has fed the hungry, educated the unlearned, sheltered the

Courtesy United Nations

In 1961, Dr. Ralph Bunche was en route to the Congo with members of Premier Adoula's party. They were aboard an aircraft taking them from Leopoldville to the U.N. base at Kitonga for peace talks with President Tshombe of Katanga Province.

Courtesy United Nations

In 1964, Dr. Bunche visited Cyprus to study the problems and needs of the United Nations truce supervision and peace force operations. Here he is touring a Turkish Cypriot refugee camp at Hamitkoy, near Nicosia.

In 1968, Dr. Bunche (center) discussed Russia's invasion of Czechoslovakia with George Ignatieff of Canada (left) and Secretary-General U Thant (right).

Courtesy United Nations

Ralph Bunche

homeless, healed the sick, and helped rid the world of some of the evils that are the root cause of war. For there can never be peace while part of the world is rich and healthy and the rest is poor and ill.

Although he has been offered many other important jobs, Dr. Bunche still holds a high position at the United Nations. He believes that only through the world organization may there be in our time "at long last full and secure peace."

Courtesy United Press International

Four

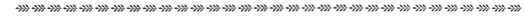

Martin Luther King Jr.

A New Weapon

In 1964, the Nobel Peace Prize was given to an American who made war not peace. But it was a very special kind of war. It was fought without guns and without bullets; the only weapons were courage, patience, and wisdom. The leader of that war was Dr. Martin Luther King Jr., and the enemy he fought was segregation.

One hundred years ago, the Civil War ended slavery in America, but in its place the white man turned to segregation. This was the system that forced the Negro to be separate and unequal. Segregation laws created two worlds, one white and one black. A Negro was born in a black hospital, lived in a black ghetto, went to a black school,

Martin Luther King Jr. appears (front row, right) as a child in an early family photograph. In the back row from left to right are: Mrs. Alberta Williams King (his mother), Martin Luther King Sr. (his father), and Jennie Williams, (his grandmother). In the front row is Alfred Daniel (his brother) and Christine (his sister).

Courtesy United Press International

worshipped in a black church, and was buried in a black cemetery. In public buildings there was one water fountain for whites, another for blacks. In buses and trains, Negroes had to sit in the back or stand.

Negroes could not get the laws changed because segregation and discrimination also kept them from voting for men who would do something for them. Finally they turned to the courts for justice. In May, 1954, the United States Supreme Court, the highest court in the land, ruled that public schools could not be segregated. Every child in America had the right to the same kind of education in the same kind of school. It was an important victory, for if segregation was forbidden in the schools, it might be forbidden everywhere. A major war against segregation was about to begin, and a young minister named Martin Luther King Jr. would come forward to lead it.

Martin Luther King Jr. was born on January 15, 1929, in Atlanta, Georgia, where his father was pastor of a large and important church. The minister's son was like any other boy, playing ball and flying kites. Once he got so angry at his younger brother that he hit him over the head with a telephone.

But when it came time to go to school, Martin had to go to a school for blacks only. The mother of two of his white friends, who were brothers, told him he couldn't play with them anymore. Segregation reached into every corner of his life. One day his father took him to a store to buy shoes. When they sat in the front of the store, the clerk told them to move to the rear. "We'll either buy shoes sitting right here," said Reverend King, "or we won't buy any of your shoes at all." The clerk refused to serve them, and they left the store.

There were many incidents like this. When Martin was a teen-ager, he was forced to give up his bus seat to a white passenger. Another time he was seated behind a curtain that divided black and white in a railroad dining car. "I felt just as if a curtain had come down across my whole life," he said.

In 1944, Martin Luther King Jr. entered Morehouse College in Atlanta. When he was a junior, he decided to become a minister. He was ordained in 1947 and became his father's assistant. The following year he graduated from Morehouse and went to Crozer Theological Seminary in Chester, Pennsylvania, on a scholarship.

While he was at Crozer, King began to wonder how good men can deal with evil. War and killing are no answer, for then the killer becomes just as evil as the man he has slain. Then one Sunday, King heard a lecture on the work of Mohandas K. Gandhi.

Gandhi was an Indian lawyer who freed his country

from British rule without firing a shot. His weapon was what he called truth force, the force of truth and love. The force of truth means you will always defeat your enemy as long as you are right and he is wrong. The force of love means you will not hurt your enemy; you would rather let him hurt you.

Gandhi taught his followers nonviolent resistance. He told them to resist and disobey unjust laws. When they were arrested, they went to jail quietly, even gladly. When the British beat and even killed them, they did not fight back.

Soon the British began to feel stupid and cruel. They did not have enough jails to hold all of the people who wanted to be arrested, and they did not like fighting men who would not fight back. Besides, people all over the world began to sympathize with the Indians. The British discovered there was nothing they could do but give the Indians their freedom. It was the greatest victory in history for a nonviolent war.

After hearing of Gandhi's work, King read every book he could find about the Indian leader. He began to wonder if the American Negro could free himself by following Gandhi's path of nonviolent resistance.

From Crozer Theological Seminary, King went to Boston University for a doctor's degree. While he was in Boston,

IN SEARCH OF PEACE

he met and married a music student named Coretta Scott. When he finished his studies, he received several job offers from different parts of the country. He had to decide whether to live in the South, where segregation was at its worst, or in the North, where it was not always as obvious. He and his wife chose the South, because that was where the blacks needed help most.

King became pastor of a church in Montgomery, Alabama. The war on segregation began there a year later.

On December 1, 1955, a Negro seamstress named Rosa Parks boarded a bus in Montgomery. She paid her fare and

Courtesy United Press International

Martin Luther King Jr. married the former Coretta Scott on June 18, 1953.

Martin Luther King Jr.

walked to the rear of the bus, where Negroes had to sit. She was happy to find an empty seat because she had worked all day and was tired.

At another stop, the bus filled with white passengers. The driver turned to the Negroes in Mrs. Parks' row and said, "Let me have those seats." The three other Negroes stood, but Mrs. Parks did not. The driver called two policemen, and Mrs. Parks was arrested for the crime of not giving up her bus seat to a white man.

But Mrs. Parks was tired, and so were the Negroes of Montgomery. They were tired of sitting in the backs of buses and standing up for white people. They were tired of unjust laws and unjust men. They were tired of not being treated as equals. They decided to fight back.

A group of Negro leaders, including Dr. King, decided to have a bus boycott. Negroes would not ride the buses until they were treated fairly. If they stayed away, the bus company would lose a lot of money. Maybe then the company would understand that black money was as good as white money and blacks were as good as whites.

The Negroes formed an organization to run the boycott and elected Dr. King president. For a year they shared car rides or walked, but they would not ride the buses. Their feet often hurt, but their backs were straight and proud.

The bus company and the city did not like the boycott, and Dr. King was arrested several times. One night, while he was at a meeting, a bomb exploded on his front porch. His wife and infant daughter were unharmed only because they had been in the back of the house.

When Dr. King came home, he found a crowd of angry Negroes armed with guns, knives, rocks, and bottles. They were ready to fight hate with hate. But Dr. King faced the mob and said, "If you have weapons, take them home. We must meet violence with nonviolence." The men put down their arms and they did not shed any blood, even though white terrorists bombed black churches and again tried to kill Dr. King and other Negro leaders.

The Negroes not only challenged segregation with their feet but in the courts. In November, 1956, the Supreme Court ruled that bus segregation in Montgomery was wrong. The laws that kept Negroes in the backs of buses were wiped out.

It was a great triumph, but the Montgomery bus boycott had done more than end just one kind of segregation. It had given the Negro a new weapon—nonviolence—and a new leader—Martin Luther King.

"I Have a Dream"

When the bus boycott began, few people had ever heard of Martin Luther King. When it ended, he was one of the best-known black leaders in the country. Newspapers, radio,

Martin Luther King Jr.

and television had spread the story of the boycott. Dr. King's arrests and the attempts to kill him made him famous. When he refused to use violence, he won much sympathy. Soon he was receiving so many awards his wife could not find place for them. He also traveled thousands of miles across the country to speak for Negro rights.

In 1958, Dr. King was nearly slain by an insane Negro woman, but he recovered. The following year he and his family moved to Atlanta, so he could work full time for civil rights. After many victories and some defeats, he decided to try a major campaign in Birmingham, Alabama, which he called "the most segregated city in America." The Negroes would force evil into the open in Birmingham so everyone could see how ugly it was. They would no longer be beaten behind closed doors where it could not be seen. They would force the authorities to beat them in public.

Demonstrations began in the spring of 1963. There were sit-ins at all-white lunch counters, kneel-ins at all-white churches, sit-ins at the all-white library, and street marches.

The local court ordered Dr. King to stop the marches, but he would not obey. He was arrested and placed in solitary confinement. President John Kennedy and Attorney General Robert Kennedy had to speak to Birmingham officials just to get permission for Dr. King to call his wife. When Dr. King was released on bail, the demonstrations continued. On May 3, black demonstrators, including children, were attacked by policemen, police dogs, and firemen with high-pressure water hoses.

With these acts, the horror of race hatred was forced into the open. Newspapers published pictures of the cruelty. People all over the world could see photographs of black children being bitten by police dogs or thrown to the ground by the pressure of the hoses. From photographs and news stories, everyone could know what the Negro suffered all of his life.

The Kennedys finally helped arrange a truce in Birmingham. The city agreed to end segregation in some public places, and Dr. King agreed to end the demonstrations. White terrorists tried to spoil the truce by attempting to kill Dr. King and his brother. But President Kennedy said the agreement was "fair and just," and he had troops ready to make sure there would be no more violence.

Dr. King had not knocked down the wall of segregation in Birmingham, but he had cracked it open. He had also succeeded in getting the full support of the federal government. When the Birmingham campaign ended, President Kennedy sent a civil rights bill to Congress that would help guarantee Negroes the rights that are given to all Americans by the Constitution.

The success in Birmingham and the President's support gave new spirit to the civil rights movement. During the summer of 1963, there were demonstrations in a thou-

From the steps of the Lincoln Memorial, Dr. King addresses the thousands of people who participated in the "March on Washington." It was here on August 28, 1963 that he delivered his famous "I have a dream" speech.

Courtesy Wide World Photos

sand American cities, and segregation ended in more places than anyone could count.

As the summer ended, there was a huge March on Washington. Some 250,000 Americans, one quarter of them white, went to the capital to ask that the Negro be given his full rights as an American. The leading speaker that day was Dr. King, who moved the crowd by repeating over and over again, "I have a dream." "I have a dream," he said, "that my four little children will one day live in a nation where they will not be judged by the color of their skin but by the content of their character."

For leading the nonviolent war against the evil of race hatred, Dr. King was given the Nobel Peace Prize in December, 1964. It was a few weeks before his thirty-sixth birthday, which made him the youngest person ever to win the award.

Less than two months after he received this honor, Dr. King was back in jail. A strong civil rights bill had been passed to help end discrimination in public places and in employment. But Dr. King felt another bill was needed to enable Negroes to vote. Every adult citizen has the right to vote. But in the South, this right was often denied Negroes by tricky laws or threats of violence.

Dr. King decided to lead a new campaign in Selma, Alabama, where only two out of every one hundred adult

Crown Prince Harold (at left) and Norway's King Olaf congratulate Martin Luther King Jr. after he received the Nobel Peace Prize in 1964.

Courtesy United Press International

Dr. Martin Luther King leads a 54-mile, five day march of civil rights demonstrators from Selma, Alabama, to the state capitol at Montgomery. The march protests Alabama's voting laws. Dr. King is easing on his shoe after a roadside rest stop during the second day of the march.

Courtesy Wide World Photos

Martin Luther King Jr.

Negroes were registered to vote. "We are going to bring a voting bill into being in the streets of Selma," he announced as demonstrations began in January, 1965. Dr. King was arrested on February 1 and released a few days later. Meanwhile, demonstrations continued. On the night of February 18, state troopers broke up a civil rights march. A young Negro was shot and killed.

To protest the murder, Dr. King called for a march to Montgomery, the state capital, some fifty miles away. On March 7, as the unarmed marchers reached the main highway, they were attacked by state troopers using tear gas, whips, and clubs. A mounted posse trampled some of the marchers under their horses' hoofs.

Although the marchers were beaten back, nonviolence won again. America was so outraged by the brutal attack that whites and blacks came to Selma from all over the land to offer their support to the marchers. One of them, a white clergyman from Boston, was beaten to death by segregationists.

Now the country was so sickened by the violence that nothing could stop the Negro cause. On March 15, President Lyndon Johnson promised to send Congress a bill that would help make it possible for every Negro to vote. "Their cause must be our cause, too," he said.

Dr. King had won what he wanted, but he decided to

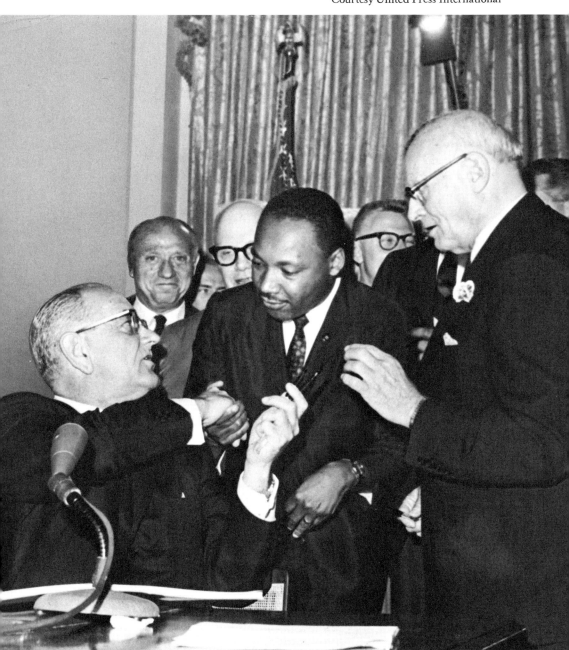
President Johnson shakes hands with Rev. Martin Luther King, Jr. after signing the Civil Rights Bill into law.

Courtesy United Press International

go ahead with the march to Montgomery to prove that Americans could peacefully demonstrate for their rights. The march was held, and on Dr. King's right as he entered the state capital was Dr. Ralph Bunche.

The voting rights bill was passed in the summer of 1965. In ten years, Dr. King, using nonviolent resistance as his only weapon, had helped to break down one hundred years of segregation and neglect. But he knew there was much more to be done.

As a world figure he worried about the problem of war and peace. "It is worthless to talk about integrating," he said, "if there is no world to integrate in." As a black leader and a national leader, he knew that no one could be free until there was an end to poverty, hunger, slums, bad schools, and poor-paying jobs. For there can be peace between races, as between nations, only if there is peace with justice.

In March, 1968, Dr. King went to Memphis, Tennessee, to support sanitation workers who were on strike. On April 4, as he stood on a balcony outside his motel room, he was shot to death by an assassin.

"I have a dream," he once said, "that one day little black boys and black girls will be able to join hands with little white boys and white girls and walk together as sisters and brothers."

Dr. King lived and died to make that dream come true.

Americans Who Have Won the Nobel Peace Prize

1906. Theodore Roosevelt
1912. Elihu Root
1919. Woodrow Wilson
1925. Charles G. Dawes
1929. Frank B. Kellogg
1931. Jane Addams and Nicholas Murray Butler
1945. Cordell Hull
1946. Emily G. Balch and John R. Mott
1950. Ralph Bunche
1953. George C. Marshall
1962. Linus C. Pauling
1964. Martin Luther King Jr.

Some Suggestions for Further Reading

Clayton, Ed. *Martin Luther King: The Peaceful Warrior.* Prentice-Hall, 1964, 1968.

Epstein, Edna. *The First Book of the United Nations.* Watts, 1963.

Galt, Tom. *The Story of Peace and War.* Crowell, 1952.

Judson, Clara Ingram. *City Neighbors, The Story of Jane Addams.* Scribner, 1951.

Judson, Clara Ingram. *Theodore Roosevelt, Fighting Patriot.* Follett, 1953.

Schlining, Paula. *The United Nations and What It Does.* Lothrop, 1962.

INDEX

Addams, Jane
 hates war, 37-38
 Theodore Roosevelt and, 37-38
 birth of, 38
 sees poverty, 39
 her stepbrother and, 39-40
 education and, 40-41
 travels abroad, 41
 shocked by suffering, 41
 visits Toynbee Hall, 43
 opens Hull House, 44-45
 refuses bribe, 46
 fights for child labor laws, 46
 founds NAACP, 46
 becomes garbage inspector, 47
 starts playgrounds, 47-48
 helps burglars, 48
 opposes World War I, 49
 starts Women's League, 51
 called traitor, 51
 wins Nobel Peace Prize, 37, 52
 dies, 53
 funeral at Hull House, 53
Addams, Mr., 38, 39, 40-41
Adirondack Mountains, 28
Africa, 34, 59
Albany, New York, 21
Albuquerque, New Mexico, 57
America. *See* United States
Arabs, 59-60, 62, 67. *See also*
 individual Arab nations
Armistice agreement, (Middle
 East), 64, 67
Asia, 32, 33, 59
Atlanta, Georgia, 75, 76, 81

Badlands (North Dakota), 23
Balance of Power, 32

Bernadotte, Count Folke, 60-63, 67
Birmingham, Alabama, 81-83
Boston, University of, 77-78
Boycott, bus, 79-80, 81
Brazil, 34
Britain/British, 60, 77
Buffalo, New York, 28
Bullfighting, 41
Bunche, Fred, 56, 58
Bunche, Olive Johnson, 56, 58
Bunche, Ralph J.
 birth of, 56
 has large "clan," 56
 grandmother's pride and, 56-57
 as newsboy, 57, 58
 sees prejudice, 57
 moves to Southwest, 57
 orphaned at thirteen, 58
 forbidden use of pool, 58
 becomes top athlete, 58
 wins scholarships, 58-59
 educated at Harvard, 59
 teaches at Howard, 59
 expert on race, 59
 serves in State Department, 59
 joins U.N. commission, 59
 goes to Palestine, 59-60
 meets Count Bernadotte, 60-62
 delayed at airport, 62
 hears of Bernadotte's death, 63
 takes over talks, 63-64
 signs armistice, 64-65
 wins Nobel Peace Prize, 65-67
 praises United Nations, 67
 continues work for peace, 67-71
 joins King march, 89
Business, regulation of, 29
Butler, Nicholas Murray, 52

California, 58, 59
Carow, Edith Kermit. *See* Roosevelt, Edith Kermit
Cease-fire (Palestine), 61
Cedarville, Illinois, 38
Chemistry prize, Nobel, 16
Chester, Pennsylvania, 76
Chicago Board of Education, 48
Chicago, Illinois, 43-44, 46, 48
Child labor, 37, 44, 46
Child labor laws, 29, 46
Civil Rights bills, 82, 84, 87-88
Civil Rights marches
  Birmingham, 81-82
  Washington, 84
  Selma, 84-87
  Montgomery, 87-89
  Memphis, 89
Civil War, 73
Coal miners, strike of, 29
Colombia, 30
Colonial peoples, definition of, 59
Courts, international, 16, 32. *See also* The Hague
Crimean War, 13
Crozer Theological Seminary, 76, 77
Cuba, 23-26

Democratic Party, 34
Demonstrations, 81-84, 86-89. *See also* Civil Rights marches and individual listings.
Detroit, Michigan, 56, 57
Desegregation, schools, 75; buses, 80; polls, 84-87
Discrimination, racial, 57, 58, 65, 73-76, 79, 84, 87
Dynamite, 11-13, 15
"Dynamite King." *See* Nobel, Alfred

Egypt/Egyptians, 63-64
Europe, 21, 41, 49, 59

Food and drug law, 29

Gandhi, Mohandas K., 76-77
Ghettos, 57, 73
Glycerine, 13. *See also* Nitroglycerine

Harvard University, 21, 22, 24, 58-59
Holdeman, George (Jane Addams's stepbrother), 39-41
Howard University, 59
Hull, Charles C., 44
Hull House, 44-46, 47-48, 53

"I have a dream . . .", 84, 89
Illinois, 38, 43, 46
Immigrants, 43-44, 57
Indemnity, definition of, 33
India/Indians, 76-77
Integration, 89
Ireland, 41
Israel/Israelis, 60, 62, 63-65, 67

Japan, 32-34
Jerusalem, 62, 63
Jews, 59-60. *See also* Israel/Israelis
Johnson, Lucy (Nana), 56-57, 58
Johnson, Lyndon, 87-88
Johnson, Olive, 56. *See also* Bunche, Olive Johnson
Johnson, Thomas Nelson, 56
Jordan, 64

Kennedy, John, 81, 82
Kennedy, Robert, 81, 82
Kettle Hill, 26, 34
Kieselgur (earth), 15
King, Coretta Scott, 78
King, Rev. Martin Luther Sr., 76
King, Martin Luther Jr.
  birth of, 75
  his family, 75

93

attends segregated schools, 75-76
denied bus seat, 76
attends colleges, 76
becomes a minister, 76
enters Seminary, 76
studies Gandhi's way, 76-77
works for doctorate, 77-78
marries, 78
made pastor in Montgomery, 78
starts bus boycott, 79-80
his house is bombed, 80
stops mob, 80
preaches nonviolence, 80-81
demonstrates in Birmingham, 81
jailed by officials, 81-82
leads Washington march, 84
"I have a dream . . .", 84, 89
wins Nobel Peace Prize, 84
campaigns for voting rights, 84-87
protests murder, 87
gets voting bill, 87-89
helps sanitation workers, 89
assassinated in Memphis, 89
Kneel-ins, 81

Labor unions, 46
Lebanon, 62, 64
Lee, Alice. *See* Roosevelt, Alice Lee
Lincoln, Araham, 38
Literature prize, Nobel, 16
London, England, 41
Los Angeles, California, 58, 65

McKinley, William, 23, 28
Madrid, Spain, 41
Malaria, 26
Massachusetts, 59
Mediation/Mediators, 32, 33-34, 48, 51, 55-56, 60-61, 62, 63-64, 67
Medicine prize, Nobel, 16
Memphis, Tennessee, 89

"Merchant of death." *See* Nobel, Alfred
Mexico, 32
Middle East War, 56, 59-60, 61-62, 63-65, 69
Montgomery, Alabama, 78-79, 80, 87, 89
Morehouse College, 76

NAACP. *See* National Association for the Advancement of Colored People
National Association for the Advancement of Colored People, 46
National parks, 30
Negroes
 slavery of, 73
 segregation of, 73-75, 78, 80
 rights denied by laws, 75-76
 discrimination against, 76-79
 marches and demonstrations by, 80-89
 civil rights bills and, 82, 84
 voting bill and, 84-87
 integration for, 89
New York City, 20, 21, 23, 65
New York, 26, 28
Nitric acid, 13. *See also* Nitroglycerine
Nitroglycerine, 13-15
Nobel, Alfred
 reads about his death, 11
 invents explosives, 11
 sells weapons, 11-13
 loves poetry, 13
 birth of, 13
 education and, 13
 joins father's business, 13
 makes nitroglycerine, 13-14
 his brother killed, 14
 discovers dynamite, 15

94

dreams of peace, 15
establishes peace prize, 16-17
dies, 16
Nobel, Immanuel, 13-14
Nobel, Oscar Emil, 14
Nobel Peace Prize
  founded by Alfred Nobel, 16-17
  first American winner, 19, 34
  first American woman winner, 37, 52
  first Negro winner, 65-67
  youngest winner, 73, 84-85.
Nonviolence, 77, 80, 84, 87, 89
North Creek, 28

Oyster Bay, Long Island, 23

Pacifism, 37, 38, 49-51
Palestine, 59-60, 61-62, 64-65, 67, 69. *See also* Middle East War
Panama Canal, 30-31
Paris, France, 15, 60
Parks, Rosa, 78-79
Peace, 13, 16-17, 32, 33-34, 37, 38, 49-51, 52, 53, 55-56, 60, 61-62, 64-65, 67, 71, 89
Peace conference, Russo-Japanese, 33-34
Physics prize, Nobel, 16
Playgrounds, public, 47-48
Portsmouth, New Hampshire, 33
Poverty, 38, 39, 41, 43-44, 46, 52, 89
Progressive Party, 34, 49

Railroad regulation, 29
Red Cross (Swedish), 62
Republican Party, 21, 26, 34, 35
Rhodes, 61-62, 63-65
Rockford Seminary, 40
Roosevelt, Alice Lee, 21
Roosevelt, Edith Kermit, 23

Roosevelt, Theodore
  birth of, 20
  childhood, 20
  education, 21, 22
  marries, 21
  joins Republican Party, 21
  State Legislator, 21
  family dies, 21
  travels West, 21-22
  adventuring years, 23
  loses mayoralty race, 23
  marries again, 23
  runs police department, 23
  Assistant Secretary of the Navy, 23
  during Spanish-American War, 24-26
  becomes hero, 26
  Governor of New York, 26-28
  Vice President, 28
  President, 28
  curbs business, 29
  supports social legislation, 29-30
  re-elected to Presidency, 29
  sportsman, 30
  protects wildlife, 30
  builds Panama Canal, 30-31
  uses world court, 32
  mediates Russo-Japanese War, 33-34, 55
  wins Nobel Peace Prize, 19, 34, 35
  joins Progressive Party, 34
  shot while campaigning, 34
  loses election, 34
  volunteers to fight, 35
  dies, 35
  opinion of Jane Addams, 37-38
  seconded by Jane Addams, 48-49
  calls pacifists cowards, 51
Rough Riders, 24-27, 34
Russia, 13, 32-34
Russo-Japanese War, 32-34, 55
Sagamore Hill, 23

Sakhalin, 33
Santiago, 25
Scott, Coretta. *See* King, Coretta Scott
Segregation, 58, 65, 73-76, 78, 80, 81-82, 84, 87, 89
Selma, Alabama, 84-87
Serot, Colonel Andre, 62-63
Settlement houses, 43. *See also* Toynbee Hall, Hull House
Siberia, 33
Sit-ins, 81
Slavery, system of, 73
Slums, 38, 39, 43-44, 46, 89
South Halsted Street, Chicago, 44
Spain, 23-26
Spanish-American War, 23-26
"Speak softly . . .", 30
Starr, Ellen Gates, 41-43, 44-45
Stockholm, Sweden, 13, 14
Supreme Court, United States, 75, 80
Syria, 64

Taft, William Howard, 34
Texas, 24
The Hague Court, 32
The Hague, Holland, 32
Toynbee Hall, 43
Truce talks, 61-62, 63-64, 65, 67, 82
Truman, Harry S, 65
Truth force (Gandhi), 77. *See also* Nonviolence
Tsar (Russian ruler), 13
Typhoid fever, 21

United States, 24, 25, 26, 29, 30, 32, 34-35, 43, 48, 49, 51, 53, 56, 65, 73, 75, 80, 81, 84, 87, 89
United Nations, 56, 59-61, 62-65, 67-71

Von Suttner, Baroness Berta, 16
Vote, right to, 37, 75, 84-87. *See also* Civil Rights bills

Wages, 29, 44, 46
War, 13, 15, 19-20, 24-26, 30-32, 34-35, 37-38, 49-51, 52, 53, 55-56, 59-60, 61-62, 64, 67, 73, 76-77, 84, 89
Washington, D. C., 52, 59
White House, 26, 30, 34, 35
Wildlife preserves, 30
Wilson, Woodrow, 34-35, 49, 51
Women, rights of, 37
Wood, Colonel Leonard, 24-25
Workers, rights of, 29, 37, 38, 46
Working conditions, 29, 37, 46
World War I, 34-35, 49, 55, 59, 60
World War II, 56, 59, 62

Yellow fever, 26